G/
CEN

Nonfiction Classics for Students, Volume 2

Staff

Editor: Elizabeth Thomason.

Contributing Editors: Reginald Carlton, Anne Marie Hacht, Michael L. LaBlanc, Ira Mark Milne, Jennifer Smith.

Managing Editor, Literature Content: Dwayne D. Hayes.

Managing Editor, Literature Product: David Galens.

Publisher, Literature Product: Mark Scott.

Content Capture: Joyce Nakamura, *Managing Editor*. Sara Constantakis, *Editor*.

Research: Victoria B. Cariappa, *Research Manager*. Cheryl Warnock, *Research Specialist*. Tamara Nott, Tracie A. Richardson, *Research Associates*. Nicodemus Ford, Sarah Genik, Timothy Lehnerer, Ron Morelli, *Research Assistants*.

Permissions: Maria Franklin, *Permissions Manager.* Shalice Shah-Caldwell, *Permissions Associate.* Jacqueline Jones, *Permissions Assistant.*

Manufacturing: Mary Beth Trimper, *Manager, Composition and Electronic Prepress.* Evi Seoud, *Assistant Manager, Composition Purchasing and Electronic Prepress.* Stacy Melson, *Buyer.*

Imaging and Multimedia Content Team: Barbara Yarrow, *Manager.* Randy Bassett, *Imaging Supervisor.* Robert Duncan, Dan Newell, *Imaging Specialists.* Pamela A. Reed, *Imaging Coordinator.* Leitha Etheridge-Sims, Mary Grimes, David G. Oblender, *Image Catalogers.* Robyn V. Young, *Project Manager.* Dean Dauphinais, *Senior Image Editor.* Kelly A. Quin, *Image Editor.*

Product Design Team: Kenn Zorn, *Product Design Manager.* Pamela A. E. Galbreath, *Senior Art Director.* Michael Logusz, *Graphic Artist.*

Copyright Notice

agency, institution, publication, service, or individual does not imply endorsement of the editors or publisher. Errors brought to the attention of the publisher and verified to the satisfaction of the publisher will be corrected in future editions.

This publication is a creative work fully protected by all applicable copyright laws, as well as by misappropriation, trade secret, unfair competition, and other applicable laws. The authors and editors of this work have added value to the underlying factual material herein through one or more of the following: unique and original selection, coordination, expression, arrangement, and classification of the information. All rights to this publication will be vigorously defended.

Copyright © 2001
The Gale Group
27500 Drake Road
Farmington Hills, MI 48331-3535

ISBN 0-7876-5381-0
ISSN 1533-7561

Printed in the United States of America.
10 9 8 7 6 5 4 3 2 1

A Room of One's Own

Virginia Woolf 1929

Introduction

A Room of One's Own is a classic text of the feminist movement. It is an expanded treatment of issues that Woolf presented in two essays she read to audiences at women's colleges in 1928. While the book is focused on women and fiction, its ideas and discussions overlap with larger questions pertinent to women's history.

At the center of the book is its famous thesis, which is echoed in the book's title. In asserting that a woman needs a room of her own to write, Woolf addresses both a historical and a contemporary question regarding women's art and their social status. The historical question is why there have been few great women writers. The contemporary question is how the number of women writers can increase. Woolf's answer—this matter of a room of one's own—is known as a "materialist" answer. That is, Woolf says that there have been few great women in history because material circumstances limited women's lives and achievements. Because women were not educated and were not allowed to control wealth, they necessarily led lives that were less publicly significant than those of men. Until the these material limitations are overcome, women will continue to achieve, publicly, less than men. Woolf's materialist thesis implicitly contests notions that women's inferior social status is a natural outcome of biological inferiority. While most people now accept the materialist position, in Woolf's time, such arguments still had to be put forward with conviction and force.

Author Biography

Adeline Virginia Woolf was born January 25, 1882, into a large family, in London, England. She grew up in an atmosphere conducive to her future career as a writer since her father, Leslie Stephen, was a respected and well-known intellectual and writer. Although she was not sent to a university as were her brothers, she was able to educate herself thoroughly by delving into the volumes of her father's vast library.

Woolf grew up during a period of intense feminist activity in London and was an active member of various women's organizations. By the time she came into her own as a writer, significant advances had been made in women's rights. By 1918, a limited franchise (vote) had been granted to women in England. Also, since World War I (1914-18) had thinned the ranks of working men, women had begun to enter the professions in large numbers.

Woolf began her career by writing literary criticism, published her first novel in 1915, and published both fiction and nonfiction copiously until her suicide in 1941. She is well known internationally for her many superb novels and collections of essays. *A Room of One's Own* (1929) and *Three Guineas* (1938) are important feminist tracts written by Woolf.

Woolf and the man who would become her husband, Leonard Woolf, were part of a group of artists, writers, and intellectuals known as the Bloomsbury Group. This group met regularly at Woolf and her brother's house in the Bloomsbury neighborhood of London before Woolf married, when she was still known as Virginia Stephen. After their marriage, the Woolfs began a small publishing house, Hogarth Press, in 1917.

Woolf suffered bouts of mental disequilibrium throughout her life. After each bout, especially as her life advanced, she worried that the next time she might not return to full sanity. It was this fear, combined with her sense of horror at the events of World War II (1939-1944), that led her to take her own life. She drowned in Sussex, England, on March 28, 1941.

Chapter One

Near the start of *A Room of One's Own*, Woolf insists that the "I" of the book is not the author, but rather a narrator persona. ("I is only a convenient term for somebody who has no real being"; "call me Mary Beton, Mary Seton, Mary Carmichael, or by any name you please.") So, it is best to say that the book opens with the narrator asserting the book's thesis, which is that for women to write fiction, they must have rooms of their own and five hundred pounds a year income (income that comes from a source other than work). The idea is that a writer needs uninterrupted time to think, and privacy, and cannot spend all of her day working if she is to have the energy and quietude of mind necessary to produce literature.

To illustrate this thesis, this chapter offers a series of anecdotes. In one of these, a lunch to which the narrator is invited at an all-male college is contrasted to a dinner at a nearby women's college. The women eat a very plain and dull dinner while the men (and their guests) are served a rich and sumptuous lunch. The chapter concludes with the narrator noting that for many centuries a great deal of money, public and private, has gone toward the education of men. In contrast, little or no money has been spent on the education of women. Woolf has made a first important point: women are impoverished and under-educated, so if there are few women writers in the history of letters, this should come as no surprise.

Chapter Two

The narrator is now in the British Library, where, she says, she will attempt to discover why it is that women are so poor and men are so rich. She consults some of the literature written about women by men, and she very quickly discerns a common theme, succinctly expressed in the title of one of the books: *The Mental, Moral, and Physical Inferiority of Women.* "England," the narrator concludes, "is under the rule of a patriarchy." What this means is that it is a society governed and controlled by men, and it is such because men are considered the superior and more capable gender. According to the narrator, men write about and constantly reiterate the inferiority of women to maintain their privileged social status and their control of power. Also, she says, by convincing themselves that women are inferior, they build up their self-confidence.

Chapter Three

This chapter begins with a paradox: How is it that history books, when they speak of women, stress how socially limited women have been, but in the literature men have written, female heroines are so interesting? The narrator partly explains this by saying that, for the most part, the history of women has been barely told. There is plenty to read about how men lived, and plenty about wars and politics, but very little about what women did. So, the gap between literature and history is partly explained by the fact that the history of women is yet to be properly written. But, on the other hand, the narrator believes that while little of detail is known of historical women, these few details are, in their general theme, accurate. That is, despite the fact that a few great women might be uncovered by historical research, the facts are that women hardly led eventful lives compared to those of men. But having touched on this idea of comparison, the narrator then suggests that one social problem women face is that their traditional roles and activities are considered less interesting than those of men.

Chapter Four

In this chapter, the narrator focuses on how the social climate affected the women of the past. Since women were supposed to be intellectually inferior, those few who did put pen to paper ended up writing a great deal of material that dwelled on their limited social roles and prospects. The narrator looks at poetry written by talented women of the seventeenth century and notes that some lines are beautiful but also that the poems as a whole tend to be marred by the writers' sense that they will not be taken seriously. Thus, a major point in this chapter is that great art is produced by those who are free in mind and spirit. If women write knowing that they will be disapproved of or laughed at, this will affect the quality of their work.

Although women were discouraged from being active in public life and letters, nevertheless, in the late eighteenth century, as the narrator says, "The middle-class woman began to write." The novel was invented, and there was a good market for anybody who could produce one. Women wrote and published quite copiously during this period. This earliest writing by women cannot be said to be great, but it created a precedent for later women to follow. And, sure enough, soon after this female entry into letters, a truly great woman writer appeared. The first great woman writer, says the narrator, was Jane Austen. She published her novels in the early decades of the nineteenth century. For the first time, a woman produced first-rate literature, which shows no evidence of a mind disabled by the thought that she will not be taken seriously.

Chapter Five

Having canvassed women's writing up to the nineteenth century in chapter four, in this chapter the narrator considers contemporary (early-twentieth-century) writing by women. She focuses on an imaginary, recently published book. Her remarks indicate that she believes that women, as a group, need another century before they will be on a par with men (individual great women writers aside). The narrator also asserts that women write differently from men in the sense that they tend to compose different types of sentences and stories. But although they write differently, she declares, this is not because they are conscious of their gender when they are writing. Rather, what makes the novel she is looking at good (if not great) is that the writer has transcended her gender in writing. Woolf's point seems to be that while women express themselves differently, what they write about, ultimately, must transcend matters strictly pertaining to gender.

Chapter Six

This book ends with the narrator looking out her window at an October day. She sees a man and a woman meeting on a nearby corner and then getting into a taxi together. This image of togetherness leads the narrator to her last major point in *A Room of One's Own*. She argues that the truly great literary mind is androgynous. That is, she says that the greatest writers are as great as they are because their minds are never wholly dominated by either masculine or feminine qualities, but by a combination of the two. A writer may be more manly than womanly, or more womanly than manly, but unless the female or male writer is at least partly his or her opposite, he or she will never be truly great. Shakespeare, Austen—all the great writers mentioned in the book—have such androgynous minds, the narrator says.

Key Figures

Jane Austen

Jane Austen (1775-1817) is one of the novelists Woolf discusses in chapter four. Austen's major novels are: *Pride and Prejudice, Emma, Sense and Sensibility, Mansfield Park,* and *Persuasion.* Austen's greatness has always been acknowledged, and ever since university literary curricula began to include literature other than the ancient classics of Greece and Rome, Austen's writing has been taught. Austen grew up and lived in the milieu of which she writes, the newly-established rural, propertied, middle-class of England.

Beadle

A beadle, historically, had a specific function in the British university system, which was namely to ensure that the protocols of the colleges were upheld, especially by their students. Today, however, they exist at few universities, and where they do, their role is largely ceremonial. For example, they might appear in traditional garb during processions. However, in Woolf's day, beadles still performed their historical function. The beadle in Woolf's book tells the narrator to remove herself from the campus lawns where, since she is a woman and not a member of the college, she is not allowed to be.

Mary Beton

Mary Beton is one of the many fictional personages in Woolf's book. She is the aunt who leaves the narrator an inheritance that allows her the independence and freedom to produce a book such as *A Room of One's Own*. However, Mary Beton's identity is complicated by an assertion made by Woolf: "Call me Mary Beton, Mary Seton, Mary Carmichael, or by any name you please."

Woolf creates a number of fictional characters and then suggests before they are fully introduced that these are names or personae that the reader can associate with the book's narrating voice. So, Mary Beton and these other Marys are both narrators and fictional personages. What Woolf accomplishes by this strategy is to turn herself into a collective entity. This is appropriate since this book pursues the collective project of women's rights.

Media Adaptations

- Patrick Garland adapted *A Room of One's Own* for the stage and directed its premiere in 1989. The play is still performed throughout the world.

Charlotte Brontë

Charlotte Brontë (1816-1855), author of *Jane Eyre* and *Villette,* amongst other novels, is, like Jane Austen, one of the greatest women writers of all time. Charlotte Brontë's most well-known book, *Jane Eyre,* is subject to some criticism from Woolf in chapter four. While Woolf acknowledges the book's many strengths, she laments those moments when the novel seems to be interrupted by overt or dogmatic pleas for women's rights. While Woolf is obviously interested in women's rights, she does not feel that art should be overtly political. Woolf uses Brontë's book to demonstrate her point that until women have achieved full rights, they will be prone to mar their art.

Mary Carmichael

Mary Carmichael, like Mary Beton and Mary Seton, is a fictional personage. She is the author of the (invented) novel that the narrator ponders and analyzes in chapter five. It is through an analysis of the story and sentences of this imagined book that

Woolf presents her theories about the differences between men's and women's art.

George Eliot

George Eliot (1819-1880), whose real name was Mary Ann (or Mary Anne) Evans, is alluded to twice. She was a leading novelist and intellectual of her time who, like many women before the twentieth century, resorted to a male pseudonym in publishing. By adopting a man's name, Eliot deflected critics' attention from her gender so that they would give her books the serious critical attention they deserved. Her most admired novels are *The Mill on the Floss, Middlemarch,* and *Daniel Deronda.* Like many Victorian novelists, Eliot is eminently concerned in her novels with moral and ethical questions, and with the individual's duties and responsibilities.

J——H——

Upon reaching the women's college in chapter one, the narrator thinks she catches sight of "J—H —herself." This is an allusion to Jane Ellen Harrison (1850-1928), a well-known classics scholar of Woolf's time. Harrison was one of the first women to graduate from Cambridge University's Newnham College where she was a lecturer from 1898 to 1922.

Mary Seton

Mary Seton is, like Mary Beton and Mary Carmichael, a persona whom the reader can assume to be a narrator of Woolf's text. She is also, like these other two Marys, a fictional personage within the book. In fact, Mary Seton is two fictional personages: In her first guise, she is a friend of the narrator in chapter one, a woman with whom the narrator chats after a dinner at the women's college. But, in this same portion of chapter one, Mary Seton is also the name given to the first Mary Seton's mother. As the mother of Mary Seton, she is a typical, traditional woman, who, unlike her daughter, did not attend college or work for women's rights.

Shakespeare's Sister

To dramatize her notion that women bestowed with artistic genius must have gone mad or at least have been terribly thwarted in earlier centuries, Woolf creates a figure she calls Shakespeare's Sister ("Judith"). Woolf then imagines Judith's life. By inventing an equally talented sister for the great British playwright, a woman who could not and did not give voice to her art, Woolf vividly communicates the great waste and loss of talent that is women's history.

William Shakespeare

William Shakespeare (1564-1616), the great British poet and playwright, is a figure whose name is synonymous with literature and artistic genius. In

A Room of One's Own, Woolf argues that Shakespeare was endowed with an androgynous (having both male and female traits) mind. Woolf holds that all great art is created by persons with androgynous minds because great art cannot be wholly masculine or feminine.

Professor von X.

Professor von X. is a composite male imagined by Woolf in chapter two. He is an extreme male chauvinist, a male academic who spends much of his time discoursing on the hows and whys of women's inferiority. He is a ridiculous and an unpleasant character who, Woolf suggests, is driven to his misogyny by personal disappointment.

Themes

Equal Opportunity

Before the mid to late eighteenth century in the West, a person was born into a social class (either the aristocracy or the peasantry, with a few steps in between). It was taken for granted that the individual's class indicated his or her worth. That is, noble men and women were just that—more noble and somehow more fully human than their humbler counterparts. But during the age of democratic revolutions (The Enlightenment), it was asserted that all men are born equal and that social and economic differences between men are the result of differences in education and opportunity. Women immediately recognized the limitations of such theories and began to assert that just as the social system had been invalidated, so should be the gender class system in which women were considered inferior. Women, they said, have as much potential as men if given education and opportunity. These basic democratic ideals constitute the origin and crux of Woolf's argument in *A Room of One's Own*. She argues that there are few great women writers in history only because women were not educated and encouraged to greatness.

Topics for Further Study

- Research Emmeline Pankhurst, the indefatigable British suffragette and feminist. What organizations and newspapers did she found or help found? What were their goals? What were her various strategies for achieving change? Write an essay that answers these questions.

- The early twentieth century was a period of fervent women's rights demonstrations across the globe. Feminists in Russia, Japan, and Mexico, for example, were extremely active at this time. Research a feminist leader of a country other than the United States or Britain and write an overview of her life and work.

- It is said that the rise of democracy in the eighteenth century and the Industrial Revolution in the nineteenth provided the combined impetus for feminist movements in Europe and the United States. Research how and why the Industrial Revolution led to changes in women's social status. Present your findings in a cause-and-effect diagram.

- Examine the relationship between the abolitionist and feminist movements in the United States in the nineteenth century. Compare and contrast this to the relationship between the civil rights and feminist movements of the 1960s. Present your findings in a graphic organizer such as a Venn diagram.

- Reread chapter three of Woolf's book. Then read Alice Walker's essay "In Search of Our Mothers' Gardens." Write a paper explaining how Walker complicates or builds on Woolf's thinking. For example, consider how Walker's ideas about art and race contest Woolf's vision of what constitutes great art and what is necessary for such art to be produced.

Difference

Woolf argues that once a woman of talent receives the same education and opportunities as her male counterpart, she is able to produce art as great as any man's. However, she also hints that this equality of opportunity does not result in the melting away of differences between male and female. This argument for difference is particularly evident in the book's final chapter in which Woolf argues that it is possible to distinguish differences between art produced by men and art produced by women. Whether Woolf believes that gender difference is a matter of biology or a result of social roles is uncertain.

Opinion Versus Truth

At the beginning of *A Room of One's Own*, Woolf says that she "should never be able to fulfill what is … the first duty of a lecturer—to hand [his or her listeners] after an hour's discourse a nugget of pure truth." Instead, she writes, all she can offer is "opinion." This humble and provisional stance is highly significant. She wants to underscore that asserting that one is in possession of the truth can be deleterious, and that it is important to distinguish theory or opinion from truth. In chapter two, Woolf points out that men, throughout history, have continuously asserted that they know the truth about women, and this truth is that women are inferior in every way to men. But, as the material circumstances of women have changed, and they have begun to do the same things men have always done, this "truth" has turned out to be only opinion or delusion. Before these men were disproved, however, many women believed this opinion to be truth, to women's great disadvantage: they internalized what men said about them.

Privilege and Entitlement

In a way, *A Room of One's Own* is a sustained polemic on the power of privilege, confidence, and entitlement. Clearly, Woolf believes that making laws that favor women can only do so much to advance their cause and social position. Equally important to this cause, however, is a woman's sense that she deserves equality, that she is as capable as men are, and that society affirms her efforts to fulfill her potential. Woolf insists that changing both men's attitudes about women and women's attitudes about themselves is crucial. A woman full of doubt about her potential will never get very far, she suggests. Likewise, women will never achieve their full potential as long as they inhabit a world in which beliefs about women's infcriority cxist.

Style

Throughout *A Room of One's Own*, Woolf interacts with her readers by addressing them as "you," as if she were giving a lecture. In fact, her first sentence pretends that the members of her audience will object to some of what she is going to say: "But, you may say, we asked you to speak about women and fiction—what has that got to do with a room of one's own?" Woolf's conversational style is a crucial component of her message. For Woolf, *how* a person delivers a lecture is just as important as its content or what it says. And the give-and-take style of *A Room of One's Own* indicates that, as a lecturer writer, Woolf does not place herself above her audience. She does not wish to present herself as a pompous know-it-all who assumes that her listeners are intellectually inferior. By acknowledging the responses of her audience, she does not assume that she is the only one in possession of ideas or knowledge. This is a book about equality, and Woolf makes sure that the way she discusses her ideas is in keeping with the ideas themselves. The style in which she presents her ideas acknowledges that her readers have minds and ideas of their own.

Tone

Much of what is presented in *A Room of One's Own* is put forward playfully or with humor, and this tone accomplishes two things. First, it guards against negative responses to its topic. Woolf knows that women's issues are touchy for many readers: many men feel threatened by feminism, and many women fear losing the love of men if they assert their rights or call themselves feminists. So, by infusing her arguments with humor, Woolf emphasizes debate over anger. Second, the easy tone sets the book apart from the typical lecture in which information is dryly imparted. By departing from typical lecture style, Woolf puts herself into a class of speakers and writers for whom lecturing and essay writing is considered art, not just a means to convey facts or ideas. The varying and often lighthearted tone of the piece is part of its attempt to be a subtle and enjoyable piece of writing, one which will entertain and delight as much as challenge and inform.

Anecdotes

Successful essays use concrete examples and specific details to illustrate general points. Woolf's essay contains a number of fictional anecdotes that serve this purpose. For example, in chapter one, Woolf wishes to dramatize the way in which women have been systematically excluded from doing certain things. She also wishes to dramatize how society favors men at the expense of women. The story of the narrator's day on a university campus illustrates these points very clearly. (The university is divided into men's and women's colleges.) The narrator describes a beadle forcing her off the grass at a men's college, and, immediately after this, being denied entrance to the men's campus library. Then, she contrasts meals eaten at this men's college and at one of the women's colleges. The narrator's forcible exclusion from real physical locations symbolizes the societal limitations imposed on women in general, and the descriptions of the contrasting meals very entertainingly illustrates how public money is lavished on men but not on women.

British Universities and Women

Cambridge and Oxford universities, each made up of various colleges, are Britain's oldest and most well-known universities. Both universities were established in the early thirteenth century although both institutions had been active as centers of learning well before their official establishment as universities. In 1869, Cambridge's Girton College became the first British college to accept women students. In 1871, Cambridge established a college specifically for women, Newnham College. Girton and Newnham Colleges are where Woolf delivered the two lectures on women and fiction that grew into *A Room of One's Own*. The "Oxbridge" of Woolf's book refers to Cambridge and Oxford, and so refers to bastions of male education in general. "Fernham," the fictional women's college depicted in Woolf's book, is an obvious allusion to Newnham.

Compare & Contrast

- **1920s:** Woolf and other British feminists such as Winifred Holtby and Rebecca West argue vigorously for women's equal opportunity in the professions and public life.

Today: Numerous female politicians, in Britain and elsewhere, have become prime ministers or presidents of their nations.

- **1920s:** The Flapper is the female icon of the day. Her short hair and simply cut, loose dresses announce a new freedom of movement and action.

  Today: Fly Girls and Riot Girls strut their stuff. These young women project independence and capability through physical fitness, skimpy clothing, and colored hair.

- **1920s:** Literature courses in British universities are geared to the education and grooming of young, upper-class men. The ancient Greek and Roman writers are taught, and a knowledge of Greek and Latin is a must.

  Today: Like all major universities around the world, British universities offer literature courses that cover all eras and languages; moreover, by the 1970s, the exclusion of literature written by women was understood to be an institutional oversight.

- **1920s:** In 1928, Britain's limited franchise (vote) for women, enacted in 1918, is extended to include all women over age 21.

Today: More so than its women, Britain's ethnic minorities, many of which come from ex-colonies, agitate for acceptance and advancement.

- **1920s:** Like pre-World War I Britain, post-World War I Britain continues its struggle to dismantle the attitudes and structures that have maintained its broad class divisions for so long.

Today: While Britain's largest class is now middle-class, nevertheless, classist attitudes and inequalities still persist.

Feminism

There have always been men and women who have decried women's second-class status in Western societies. But feminism as a viable and broad-scale movement did not take off until democratic ideals pervaded the West during the eighteenth century. Since that time, feminist activity has been consistent, though sometimes more vigorous and sometimes less so. Mary Wollstonecraft, a British woman who was inspired by the events of the democratic revolutions, published the first major feminist tract in English, *A Vindication of the Rights of Women,* in 1797. Feminism gathered force during the nineteenth century as women entered public life as factory workers during the course of the Industrial Revolution. The philosopher and economist John Stuart Mill's *The Subjection of Women* (1869) was an influential British feminist tract of the mid-nineteenth century. Feminism achieved its first major gain in the West when women were granted the vote in 1918 in Britain and in 1920 in the United States. However, since women's social status and opportunities continued to lag behind those of men during the twentieth century, a new women's rights movement was forged in the 1960s.

British Suffragettes

The early decades of the twentieth century, like the 1960s and 1970s, were years of major, particularly intensive feminist action throughout the world. The rise of socialist philosophies, of which a major component is the equality of the sexes, gave impetus to feminist demonstrations in places as diverse as Japan, Mexico, and Russia. Things were no different in the United States and Britain, and the feminists of London, in particular, were known for the vigor and militancy of their actions. Feminists were most often referred to as suffragettes at this time because their primary goal was to gain the vote, or suffrage, for women. And no suffragettes were more creative in their methods than the followers of Emmeline Pankhurst, who was one of the principal British feminist organizers of the time. British suffragettes would invade parliamentary sessions and create disturbances, march down streets at inconvenient times to disrupt business, or, more typically, engage in peaceful demonstrations. One demonstration that took place in 1908 in London's famous Hyde Park attracted almost half a million people. Some of the more militant acts engaged in by turn-of-the-century feminists were stone throwing and hunger strikes.

World War I

The connection between early-twentieth-century British feminism and World War I (1914) is a complex and mixed one. First, the start of this terrible war cut short feminist activity which was, at the time, vigorous. It seemed, before the start of the war, that women were on the verge of gaining the vote in England. But once the war began, few people had time to attend to the problems of women. Instead, everybody, including feminists, threw themselves into the war effort. These women became nurses, ambulance drivers, intelligence operatives, and the like. In addition, since so many men were off fighting, women were called to take their places in the regular work force. And since this war resulted in the deaths of so many men, many of these same women were able to keep these jobs once the war was over. So, despite the fact that the war cut short organized feminist activity, it ended up advancing women's cause in the long run, because it facilitated women's entry into the professions. Also, since women contributed to the war effort so valiantly and extensively, Parliament passed a bill giving certain women the vote the very year the war ended (the Parliamentary Reform Act of 1918).

Critical Overview

A Room of One's Own is widely acknowledged to be a major work of feminist thought, just as many of Woolf's novels are considered major works of English-language fiction. *A Room of One's Own* is especially admired for its unparalleled breadth of inquiry and for the power of its metaphors. Its story of "Shakespeare's sister," its notion of "a room of one's own," and its idea that women "think back through [their] mothers," for example, are staple phrases of post-1950s feminist dialogues. The book's reputation rests not only on the way in which it captures the concerns of the author's own time, but also for the way in which it anticipates so much of the thinking and writing of contemporary feminism and literary theory.

Numerous feminists claim that *A Room of One's Own* is the single most important twentieth-century feminist text. In 1983, for example, in "'I Have Bought My Freedom': The Gift of A Room of One's Own," Patricia Joplin states, "It would be hard to find any major work of American feminist theory, particularly literary theory, that is not to some degree indebted to *A Room of One's Own.*" Jane Gallop, in *Around 1981: Academic Literary Theory,* calls Woolf's book "the founding book of feminist literary criticism." In fact, the book that launched academic feminism after World War II, Kate Millet's *Sexual Politics,* is said to be closely modeled after Woolf's book.

While no feminist dismisses Woolf's book outright, numerous theorists question or contest some of the arguments presented in the book. For example, Alice Walker's "In Search of Our Mothers' Gardens" questions some of the author's assumptions and points to alleged conceptual limitations. Walker, an African-American feminist and fiction writer, says that Woolf's focus on "high art" is a classist position. For Walker, many poor women (i.e., not just women with rooms of their own and inheritances) produce great art; one must simply look "low" as well as "high." By looking "low," Walker means that quilts, beautiful gardens, and other art forms should be valued as much as printed books and formal paintings. Other feminists question the validity of Woolf's notion that there is a difference between men's and women's literature. As Sandra Gilbert and Susan Gubar point out, there seems to be no empirical truth to the claim that women's sentences are different from men's. In their book *No Man's Land: The War of the Words,* they suggest instead that Woolf is presenting a "fantasy about a utopian linguistic structure" that does not describe women's language, but rather their *"relation"* to language.

Sources

[This text has been suppressed due to author restrictions]

Gallop, Jane, *Around 1981: Academic Feminist Literary Theory,* Routledge, 1992.

Gilbert, Susan M., and Sandra Gubar, *The War of the Words,* Vol. I of *No Man's Land: The Place of the Woman Writer in the Twentieth Century,* Yale University Press, 1989.

Joplin, Patricia, "'I Have Bought My Freedom': The Gift of *A Room of One's Own,*" in *Virginia Woolf Miscellany 21,* Fall 1983, pp. 4-5.

Millet, Kate, *Sexual Politics,* Virago, 1969.

Walker, Alice, "In Search of Our Mothers' Gardens," in *In Search of Our Mothers' Gardens: Womanist Prose,* Harcourt Brace Jovanovich, 1983.

Further Reading

Bell, Clive, *Old Friends,* Harcourt, Brace & Co., 1956.

> This is a description of the Bloomsbury Group, of which Woolf was a part, by one of its members. Bell married Woolf's sister, Vanessa (Stephen) Bell, who was a painter.

Evans, Nancy Burr, "The Political Consciousness of Virginia Woolf: *A Room of One's Own* and *Three Guineas,*" in *New Scholar,* Vol. 4, 1974, pp. 167-80.

> This is an analysis of Woolf's politics and feminism based on a reading of Woolf's two feminist books.

Fussell, Paul, *The Great War and Modern Memory,* Oxford University Press, 1975.

> This book is about World War I, its impact on British life, and the literature some of its soldiers produced.

Lee, Hermione, *Virginia Woolf,* Alfred A. Knopf, Inc., 1996.

> This is a recent biography of the author.

Woolf, Virginia, *The Years*, Harcourt, Brace, Jovanovich, 1965.

Woolf's eighth novel, first published in 1937, chronicles the lives of various members of a family through many decades.